W9-BAT-450

DATE DUE

THE DIVERSITY OF LIFE

FROM SINGLE CELLS TO MULTICELLULAR ORGANISMS

Robert Snedden

Series Editor
Andrew Solway

Heinemann Library
Chicago, Illinois

Designed by Paul Davies and Associates
Illustrations by Wooden Ark
Originated by Ambassador Litho Ltd.
Printed by Wing King Tong in Hong Kong

07 06 05 04 03
10 9 8 7 6 5 4 3 2

Library of Congress Cataloging-in-Publication Data
Snedden, Robert.
   The diversity of life : from single cells to multicellular organisms /
Robert Snedden.
         v. cm. -- (Cells & life)
Includes index.
Contents: A dazzling diversity -- What's in a name? -- Living kingdoms
-- All together now -- Mutations -- Genetic drift -- Natural selection
-- Adaptation -- Ripples in the gene pool -- Speciation -- Simple
beginnings -- A tour of the kingdoms -- Protistans -- Fungi -- Plants --
Plant evolution -- Animals -- A brief history of life -- The end of the
line -- The threat to diversity.
   ISBN 1-58810-673-X (HC), 1-58810-935-6 (Pbk.)
   1. Biological diversity--Juvenile literature. [1. Biological
diversity.] I. Title. II. Series.
   QH541.15.B56 S64 2002
   570--dc21
                             2001008582

Acknowledgments
The author and publishers are grateful to the following for permission to reproduce copyright material:
p.4 D.B. Fleetham/Oxford Scientific Films; p. 5 Digital Vision; p. 6a D. Fleetham/Oxford Scientific Films; p. 6b T. Bernhard/Oxford Scientific Films; p. 7 F. Schneidermeyer/Oxford Scientific Films; p. 9 K. Lounatmaa/Science Photo Library; p. 11 M. Tibbles/Oxford Scientific Films; p. 12/Garden Matters; p. 13 B. Kenmey/Oxford Scientific Films; p. 15 Science Photo Library; p. 16 K. Willson/Corbis; pp. 17, 26, 28 J. Burgess/Science Photo Library; p. 18 N. Rosing/Oxford Scientific Films; p. 19 L. Bush/Link; p. 20 J.B. Blossom/Survival Anglia; p. 21 S. North/Garden Matters; p. 22 G. Murti/Science Photo Library; p. 23 D. Phillips/Science Photo Library; p. 24 G. Ochoki/Science Photo Library; p. 25 A. and H-F Michler/Science Photo Library; p. 27 J. Howard/Science Photo Library; p. 29 I. West/Oxford Scientific Films; p. 30 J.C. Revy/Science Photo Library; p. 31 J. Watts/Science Photo Library; p. 32 B. Watts/Science Photo Library; p. 33 P. Goetgheluck/ Science Photo Library; p. 35 S. Meyers/Oxford Scientific Films; p. 36 Photo disc; p. 37 B. Goodale/Oxford Scientific Films; p. 39 David Dilcher and Ge Sun, University of Florida; p. 40 S. Stammers/Science Photo Library; p. 41 C. Palek/Oxford Scientific Films; p.42 G. Bernard/Science Photo Library; p. 43 Garden & Wildlife Matters;

Cover photograph reproduced with permission of Science Photo Library/Andrew Syred.

Our thanks to Richard Fosbery for his comments in the preparation of this book, and also to Alexandra Clayton.

Every effort has been made to contact copyright holders of any material reproduced in this book.
Any omissions will be rectified in subsequent printings if notice is given to the publisher.

Some words are shown in bold, **like this.** You can find out what they mean by looking in the glossary.

Contents

1 Life's Dazzling Diversity

Diversity is the wealth of life. It is what gives life its power to survive. Several times in Earth's long history, life has been dealt serious harm. At the end of the **Permian period** 250 million years ago, 95 percent of the **species** then living on Earth became extinct. Sixty-five million years ago, another catastrophe wiped out the dinosaurs and many marine creatures. Yet life bounced back and diversified once more. Today, life in a dazzling variety of shapes and sizes swarms the planet.

It is remarkable that despite the incredible variety of life, all living things at the most basic level are similar. Virtually all life is made up of simple units called cells. All cells work in more or less the same way, and they are all constructed from more or less the same chemicals. Cells need energy, which they must get in some way from their surroundings. They also need raw materials with which to rebuild, repair, and reproduce themselves. Finally, all cells respond in some way to their environments.

Ordering living things

No one is sure how many millions of different species of organisms there may be sharing this planet. New ones are discovered and named all the time. Even in well-known groups of animals, such as birds, about three new species are discovered and named each year. Many more insects and smaller organisms are added each year as well.

On land, the greatest concentration of life's diversity is in rain forests. Coral reefs such as this one are the rain forests of the ocean. They are full of life forms, ranging from microscopic plankton to incredible sharks.

Organizing all the millions of living things into groups helps us make sense of the tremendous variety of life. It also enables us to make connections between living things that at first may seem very different. The science of naming and identifying organisms is called **taxonomy.**

Scientists organize all living things into related groups in an orderly arrangement known as scientific classification. Seven groups make up a system in scientific classification. At the bottom of the scale, all living things are placed in basic groups called species. A species is a group of organisms that can breed together to produce offspring capable of reproducing.

Going up the scale, similar species are placed in a group called a **genus.** All the species in a genus have many features in common. Closely related genera are grouped into **families;** families are placed into larger groups called **orders;** orders are grouped into **classes;** classes are grouped into **phyla;** and phyla are grouped into **kingdoms.** Kingdoms are the largest groups. Animals and plants are the most familiar kingdoms, but there are several others.

Pinning down the tiger

Looking at the classification of an organism helps make scientific classification clearer.

A tiger belongs to the kingdom Animalia. Within this kingdom, it is classified in the phylum Chordata (chordates) and the subphylum Vertebrata (vertebrates), because it has a bony vertebral column, or backbone. A tiger is a mammal (class Mammalia), meaning it is a fur-covered vertebrate that feeds its young breast milk. It is a member of the order **Carnivora,** or carnivores. Tigers belong to the family Felidae (cats) and the genus *Panthera,* the big cats. Its species name is *tigris.*

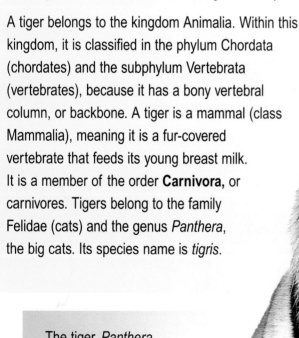

The tiger, *Panthera tigris,* is classified in the animal kingdom.

2 Classification Schemes

Ordering living things into groups is not an easy task. For any classification system to be useful, it must group things in a sensible way. For instance, say you were organizing the books in a library. If you grouped the books according to the color of their covers or to their size, your system would not be of much use if you wanted to find a book on a particular subject. To make the books easy to find, you would want to use a classification system based on the subject matter of the book. For living things, the most useful classification system is based on how closely organisms are related.

Dolphins and sharks look similar in many ways. A dolphin certainly looks more like a shark than a deer or a sheep. But dolphins are much more closely related to hoofed mammals than they are to sharks. The apparent similarities between the two animals come from their similar lifestyles and environments, rather than from similar origins.

How closely humans are related to each other depends on how long ago they had a common ancestor. If you have a brother or sister, your common ancestors are very recent. They are your parents. Cousins are less closely related because their common ancestors are their grandparents, on either their mother's or father's side of the family. In a similar way, closely related **species** have a relatively recent common ancestor, while for less closely related species the common ancestor is farther in the past.

Comparing species

For most species, it is not possible to find out enough about their past to identify common ancestors. Instead, scientists compare different characteristics of each species to try and determine the relationships among them. In the past, scientists were able to look only at the anatomy, or structure, of organisms and at their physiology, or how the different parts of the animal work.

Today's scientists can look more deeply to find the relationships among living organisms. They can look, for example, at an organism's biochemistry—the chemicals that make up its cells and the reactions that occur in these cells. One of the reasons for separating different groups of fungi, for example, is based on the structure of their cell walls.

The American robin, *Turdus migratorius*, is more closely related to British thrushes and blackbirds than to the British robin.

What's in a name?

The common names that we give to living things do not clearly identify them for scientific purposes. Common names are not very precise. *Robin,* for instance, is the name for one bird in North America and for an entirely different one in Britain. Also, *robin* is the English common name. Someone who speaks French, Japanese, or Swedish would use a different name. Most living things, such as many of the fungi, do not have a common name at all.

For biologists, it is essential that there be an internationally recognized system for naming organisms. The system used is the binomial nomenclature system. *Binomial* means "two names." Each species has a first name that reveals its **genus** and a second name that identifies its species. The names are in Latin. In this binomial nomenclature, the American robin is called *Turdus migratorius*, while the British robin is called *Erithacus rubicola*.

Carolus Linnaeus

Eighteenth-century Swedish naturalist Carl von Linné, known by his Latin name of Carolus Linnaeus, developed a system for naming and classifying organisms. Linnaeus's book, *Systema Naturae* (1735), outlined his system of classification for plants, animals, and **minerals,** and a later book revealed a more detailed classification for plants. Although many of the details of Linnaeus's system have been replaced, his system has remained the basis of modern **taxonomy.**

Living Kingdoms

One of the earliest classifications of the living world divided it into two **kingdoms**: plants and animals. It was developed in the eighteenth century.

For two centuries this two-kingdom scheme was accepted, despite the problems of deciding where to put the large numbers of bacteria and other microorganisms revealed by the microscope. Then in 1969, ecologist Robert Whittaker suggested that the world's organisms should be divided among five kingdoms rather than two. These are the **Monera, Protista,** Plantae, Fungi, and Animalia.

Monera

Monera is the kingdom of bacteria. They are single-celled organisms, and their cells are simpler than those of all other living things. Bacterial cells have no obvious internal structure and no nucleus. They are **prokaryote** cells. Despite their apparent simplicity, bacteria are a diverse group of organisms. They are found in almost every place on Earth, from deep beneath the ocean to high in the atmosphere. Some bacteria can make their own food using light energy, just as plants can. Others are essential decomposers of **organic** wastes.

Protista

Most of the **species** in this group are single-celled organisms. Some scientists include seaweeds and other **algae** here, but others place them in the plant kingdom. The cells of Protistans are more complex than those of bacteria. They contain smaller structures called **organelles** within them. The largest of these organelles is the **nucleus,** which contains the cell's **genetic material.** This type of cell is described as **eukaryote.**

This diagram shows the five major kingdoms of life.

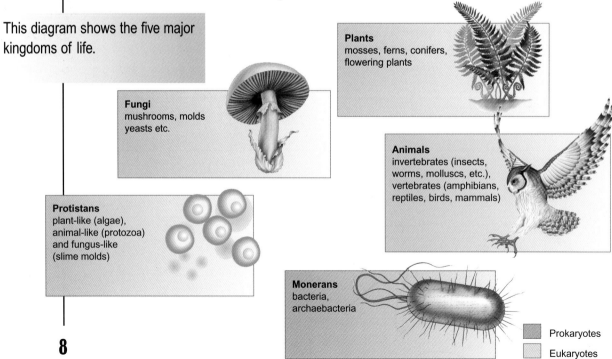

Plants
mosses, ferns, conifers, flowering plants

Fungi
mushrooms, molds yeasts etc.

Animals
invertebrates (insects, worms, molluscs, etc.), vertebrates (amphibians, reptiles, birds, mammals)

Protistans
plant-like (algae), animal-like (protozoa) and fungus-like (slime molds)

Monerans
bacteria, archaebacteria

Prokaryotes

Eukaryotes

Plantae

Plants are multicellular eukaryotes. Plants produce their own food by harnessing the energy of sunlight in a process called **photosynthesis.** Organisms that can make their own food in this way are called **autotrophs.** All cells have a thin outer membrane, but plants also have a thicker, rigid cell wall. Plant cells contain **chloroplasts,** the organelles in which photosynthesis takes place. Plants are of vital importance to most of the rest of the living world. The food they make becomes part of the plants themselves, which provide food for plant-eating animals. These in turn are food for other animals. In addition to being food for the living world, plants also produce oxygen during photosynthesis, which is necessary for the survival of most other organisms.

Fungi

Multicellular eukaryote organisms known as the fungi were once lumped together with the plants. However, unlike plants, fungi cannot make their own food. They are **heterotrophs** and need to consume other organisms to get their nutrients. Many species of fungi are important decomposers, while others are **parasites.** The fungi include mushrooms, yeasts, and molds.

Animalia

Animals are multicellular eukaryotes. They also are heterotrophs. Some animals are **herbivores,** others are **carnivores,** and some are parasites. Animal cells differ from plant cells in that they do not have an outer cell wall. More than a million species of animals have been identified.

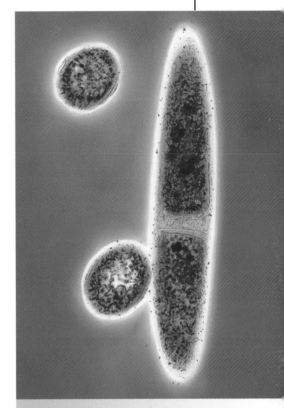

The **archaebacteria** thrive in extreme conditions, such as high temperatures or extreme salinity, or saltiness. This photo shows the bacterium *Methanospirillum* dividing. Magnification approx. x 29,000.

A sixth kingdom?

In the 1970s, scientists studying bacteria used new techniques to study the genetic material of some of these organisms. They discovered such differences among some of the bacteria that it was suggested that the kingdom Monera be divided in two. Many biologists now support the idea that bacteria should be split into two separate kingdoms, the eubacteria (true bacteria) and the archaebacteria. The archaebacteria are as distinct from eubacteria as they are from eukaryote cells. It is widely believed that archaebacteria were the ancestors of the eukaryotes many millions of years ago.

3 Populations and Genes

A **population** of living organisms is a group of individuals of the same **species** living within a given area. All the members of a population will usually look the same. Their bodies are put together in the same way, their **organs** work in the same way, and their cells all work in the same way. In addition, the members all behave in more or less the same way.

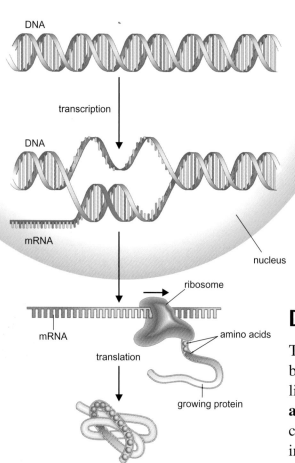

DNA

transcription

DNA

mRNA

nucleus

ribosome

mRNA

amino acids

translation

growing protein

completed protein

DNA molecules carry a code within their structure. Messenger RNA (mRNA) carries one section of this code, the **gene** for a particular protein, to **organelles** called ribosomes that are outside the **nucleus.** The ribosomes then assemble the protein according to the coded instructions.

However, the individuals within a population are not all exactly the same. No two leopards, for instance, will have exactly the same spots. Some plants in a population might be better able to resist drought than others. And while most people can run, only a very few can run fast enough to compete in the Olympics. Wherever we look in the natural world, we see populations with characteristics in common that identify them as a group and individuals within these populations that differ from each other. Individuals in a species vary in almost every way possible. But just how do these endless variations come about?

DNA

The reason why all the members of a species are basically the same and yet individually different lies in a substance called **DNA (deoxyribonucleic acid).** DNA is found in every living cell in strands called chromosomes. It is like a chemical instruction manual. Built into DNA's structure are coded instructions for making **proteins.** Proteins are the building blocks and workhorses of the cell. Some proteins are essential parts of the cell's structure. Others are **enzymes,** substances that control the endless flow of chemical reactions in the living cell. Each reaction that takes place in the cell has its own specific enzyme, and because the enzymes control the reactions, they effectively control the cell and the way it develops. Different combinations of enzymes, used in different ways, produce different characteristics in cells and in the organisms they are part of.

A segment of DNA that carries a protein-building instruction is called a gene. All of the individuals in a population have, by and large, the same number and kinds of genes. However, individuals within a population may have different versions of the same gene. Whether you have brown eyes or blue eyes depends on which versions of the genes that control eye color you possess. There can be many varieties of each gene, so there are a huge number of ways in which different versions of thousands of genes can combine to produce a different mix of characteristics in each individual.

Inherited genes

Organisms inherit their genes from their parents. Half the genes come from the father and half come from the mother. In **sexual reproduction,** the male and female both produce special cells, the male and female sex cells, which contain half the normal number of chromosomes. A sex cell from the male and a sex cell from the female fuse, or join together, to produce a new individual. This process is known as fertilization.

Fertilization is a random event. There is no way to predict which sex cell from a parent will successfully fuse with a sex cell from the other parent. The possible number of combinations that can occur from this shuffling of the genetic deck of cards is truly mind-boggling. There are 10^{600} possible gene combinations that can occur in humans. That is a 1 with 600 zeroes after it. If you consider that there are 6,000,000,000 (6 billion) or so people alive today, you can see that it is highly unlikely that there is anyone anywhere who is just like you (unless of course you are an identical twin).

A green turtle (*Chelonia mydas*) lays her eggs. Each egg develops from a fertilized egg cell that contains **genetic material** from both the female and the male.

Mutations

Combinations of different **genes** might seem to offer all the variation a **population** could ever need. However, they are just new combinations of genes that already exist. To explain the diversity of life, there needs to be some way in which new characteristics can arise and produce new types of organisms.

Almost every time a cell divides, the **DNA** it contains is copied perfectly. Occasionally, however, a mistake is made, and the DNA is altered in some way. The altered genes that result are called **mutations.** Mutations are the only way in which new genes can appear.

Effects of mutations

We cannot predict when a mutation will appear. Nothing actually causes most mutations.

A single mutation can cause a change in the color of an organism. The mutation could alter a gene which codes for an **enzyme** that controls the making of a particular pigment. In this bluebell (*Hyacinthoides nonscripta*), a mutation has resulted in white flowers.

They are simply random copying errors that occur when DNA is duplicated. However, each gene has its own mutation rate, which is the probability that it will mutate during DNA replication. We can expect that a mutation will occur between every 100,000 and 1,000,000 times a gene is copied. Such a slow rate means that in slow-breeding populations such as humans, mutations are rarely seen. In a large, fast-reproducing population such as some bacteria that can divide every twenty minutes in ideal conditions, mutations and variations can arise fairly often.

Most mutations are damaging. Usually, a cell that has mutated genes dies because it cannot function properly. However, sometimes a mutated cell survives. In most cases this has little or no effect, because it is only one cell among billions. But, it could lead to the formation of a cancer. And if a mutation occurs in a sex cell, there is a chance that it will be passed on to the next generation. Such mutations can cause serious problems. Sickle cell disease is a genetic blood disease that is thought to have originally been produced by a mutation.

Some mutations are neutral. They have neither a good nor a bad effect. On very rare occasions, a mutation can be beneficial and give an organism an advantage over the others in its population. If the organism with the mutation can pass this benefit on to its offspring, they too will have this advantage. The mutation will gradually become more common until, after many generations, most members of the **species** have it. This is the basis of **evolution.**

Close relations

Scientists can use mutations to establish how closely related species are to each other. There are some genes that are found in just about all living things. Some examples are the genes that code for the enzymes involved in **respiration.** The more closely related two species are, the more likely it is that these particular genes are the same. For example, comparing humans and chimpanzees may show no differences at all in the structure of one of these genes. However, a gene that codes for one of these enzymes in mushrooms has around 50 differences when compared to its equivalent in humans. What this tells us is that humans and chimps shared a common ancestor fairly recently, perhaps within the last few million years. However, the lines of ancestry that gave rise to humans and mushrooms went their separate ways hundreds of millions of years ago.

It is possible to use the average mutation rate to work out roughly when the common ancestor of two species lived. Neutral mutations are those that have no effect on survival. They occur in the DNA at a regular rate, like the ticking of a molecular clock. Counting back the ticks allows scientists to calculate roughly when a particular species appeared. Results from one such study suggest that raccoons, giant pandas, and bears had a common ancestor that lived around 40 million years ago.

The red panda looks like a close relative of the giant panda, but gene studies have shown that it is closer to the raccoon. All had a common ancestor, however, that lived 40 million years ago.

13

Darwin's Great Idea

Mutations, random changes in **genes,** can on rare occasions result in changes that are of benefit to an organism. Such beneficial mutations are important parts of the process of **evolution,** by which **species** change and adapt over time. But how exactly do genetic changes act to change a whole **population?**

No matter how successful an organism becomes, it is going to face challenges to its survival. For example, a population that is successful and reproduces rapidly will eventually run out of space and food if it isn't held back in some way. If the population increases beyond the ability of the environment to support it, the individuals in the population will have to compete with each other for space, food, and the chance to breed.

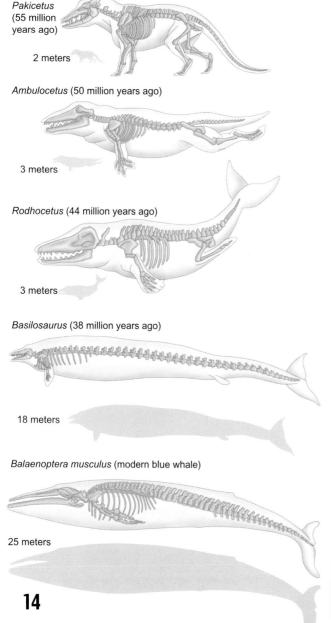

Pakicetus (55 million years ago)

2 meters

Ambulocetus (50 million years ago)

3 meters

Rodhocetus (44 million years ago)

3 meters

Basilosaurus (38 million years ago)

18 meters

Balaenoptera musculus (modern blue whale)

25 meters

Although all the members of a population have the same types of genes, we have seen that there is variety within those genes. Those individuals best equipped to survive in their environment are the ones that are most likely to have offspring. A beneficial mutation is one that gives an advantage in the competition for resources such as food and space.

For example, a plant-eating population of animals might be well adapted to its environment. If a new predator moves into the area, those members of the population best adapted to deal with it will be the ones most likely to survive and reproduce. A beneficial mutation in this situation might be one that helps an individual run faster. Over time, the whole population will become swift runners, because the slower animals will be killed by the predators before they can reproduce.

Evidence from **fossils** gives biologists a fairly good idea of how the whale has evolved over time to become better adapted to its environment and lifestyle.

What this means is that those genes that offer the greatest advantage will increase in the population, while those that leave the individual disadvantaged will decrease. The individuals that possess beneficial genes are more likely to reproduce successfully. This process is known as natural selection.

Natural selection

The theory of evolution by natural selection was first outlined in the nineteenth century by Charles Darwin and separately by Alfred Russel Wallace. Darwin saw that populations in nature have the ability to reproduce and increase their numbers over time. Indeed, more offspring are produced than will survive to reproduce. Darwin was inspired by reading *An Essay on the Principle of Population* by Thomas Malthus. Malthus argued that the human population could not go on increasing in size for ever, because sooner or later it would become unable to feed itself. The size of the population would eventually be checked by famine, disease, or war.

Charles Darwin first began to develop his theory of natural selection during a voyage around the world on the survey ship, HMS *Beagle*.

Darwin had the idea of applying Malthus's ideas to other organisms. He realized that other living things also have to compete for resources, both with other organisms and with members of their own species. Within a particular population there are a range of characteristics, and some are more beneficial than others at helping individuals survive and reproduce. A population made up of such diverse individuals has the potential to evolve. This is possible because those organisms that have the greatest likelihood of surviving have the greatest chance of reproducing. However slight an advantage might be, over time it will be selected in favor of other characteristics. Natural selection, in other words, is simply what results from the differences among individuals. Some will survive to reproduce because they are better suited to their environment. This is sometimes called survival of the fittest.

Because Darwin knew nothing of genetics, he had no idea of how these variations among individuals might have arisen. Around the time Darwin was presenting his ideas, an Austrian monk named Gregor Mendel was conducting experiments with pea plants that would become the foundations of the modern science of genetics. Unfortunately, Mendel's work was overlooked until twelve years after Darwin's death.

Adaptation

The changes brought about in **populations** as a result of natural selection are called adaptations. A population adapts to its environment in response to an ever-changing series of pressures, such as changes in climate and competition from other organisms. For example, the pattern of stripes on a tiger are an adaptation that allows this predator to get close to its prey without being seen. The long legs of an antelope are an adaptation that gives it the best chance of escape from a predator. The spines on a cactus are an adaptation that prevents thirsty animals from drinking all the plant's stored water.

Mimicry

One of the best examples of adaptation at work is mimicry. Some organisms imitate the coloration or appearance of a **species** that is distasteful or even hazardous to predators. Some flies, for example, have evolved to be similar in appearance to wasps or bees. The bee fly has no sting, but a predator, fooled by the adaptation, thinks twice before attacking the bee fly. The bee fly then has a better chance of escaping being eaten. The idea is that natural selection has been at work here, with birds in the role of selectors. Those bee flies that looked least like bees were eaten, while those that looked most like them were not. The genetic makeup of the bee fly population gradually shifted to favor the mimics.

This fly (*Volucella inanis*) has no sting and presents no danger to predators. However, its wasplike appearance deters predators from trying to eat it. Magnification approx. x 40

Adaptive radiation

The adaptations in living organisms are largely determined by their environment. Many new species can evolve when individuals of a single ancestral population spread out to take advantage of new **habitats.** This process is known as **adaptive radiation.**

One example of adaptive radiation occurs when a small population reaches an isolated habitat, such as a remote island, and over time it adapts to take advantage of all the habitats on the island.

Darwin's finches

When Charles Darwin was a young man, he sailed around the world as the ship's geologist and naturalist on the survey ship, HMS *Beagle*. During the voyage, the *Beagle* visited the Galapagos Islands, where Darwin observed one of the most famous examples of adaptive radiation.

There are thirteen species of finch on the Galapagos Islands, all similar but each with a particular adaptation. One species has a large, strong bill adapted for cracking seeds, another has a slender bill adapted for probing for insects. One species has even learned to use a cactus spine as a probe to reach insects hidden from sight in tree bark.

Darwin suggested that the different kinds of finch had arisen through adaptive radiation. There are no other bird species on the islands to compete with the finches, so they have taken on the roles that in other places are filled by birds such as woodpeckers and warblers. Darwin guessed that one species of finch colonized the islands thousands of years ago and gave rise to the variety of species that exist there now.

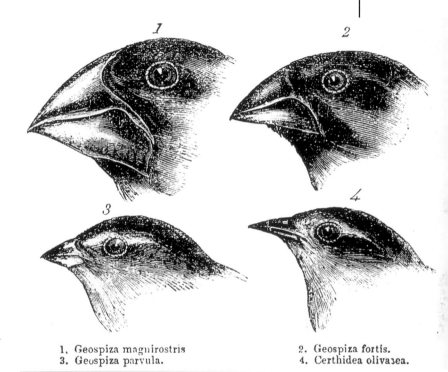

1. Geospiza magnirostris
3. Geospiza parvula.

2. Geospiza fortis.
4. Certhidea olivaJea.

Darwin's drawing showing the different beak shapes of the Galapagos finches.

Another form of adaptive radiation occurs when the dominant species, or group of species, in an area becomes extinct for some reason. Probably the best known example of this occurred about 65 million years ago, at the end of the Cretaceous period. At this time, dinosaurs were the dominant large animals on land. Then some global event, perhaps a large **asteroid** crashing into Earth, led to the disappearance of dinosaurs. Their place as the dominant large animals was taken by mammals. Mammals underwent a spectacular process of expansion into different environments.

Genes in Populations

All the different varieties of **genes** present in a **population** together make up its gene pool. The gene pool of a large population of varied individuals is huge. It includes many different versions of the different types of genes. However, a small population of individuals has a smaller gene pool. This lack of diversity may make the population vulnerable to any changes in its environment.

The bottleneck effect

The bottleneck effect occurs when large numbers of a population are destroyed by some natural disaster. As a result, the genetic diversity of the population is reduced because its gene pool has been diminished. Which gene variations are lost is a matter of chance.

Inbreeding occurs when closely related individuals with many genes in common mate with one another. This is likely to occur in a population whose numbers have been reduced as a result of the bottleneck effect. Inbreeding can lead to all the members of a population having the same genes for particular characteristics. Once again, variety is lost and the population becomes less able to adapt to changing circumstances.

The present-day population of cheetahs is descended from just a few survivors from the nineteenth century. The population has a very limited amount of genetic variation because it is descended from such a small number of ancestors.

An endangered **species** can find itself in great trouble because of the effects of bottlenecks and inbreeding. One example of these effects is the African cheetah. About 10,000 years ago, cheetahs probably came close to extinction. As a result, the modern cheetah population is descended from only a few hundred individuals. Cheetah populations fell drastically once more in the nineteenth century.

Although the cheetah's numbers have now recovered, inbreeding has led to a situation in which today's cheetahs all have a very similar genetic makeup. One **mutation** that became established in the population affects fertility. Most male cheetahs have a low sperm count and 70 percent of the sperm produced is abnormal. This means that there is a low reproduction rate, which threatens the future survival of the species. Zoos that breed cheetahs keep records of the genetic history of each individual. They use this information to help avoid inbreeding as much as possible.

Founder effect

A particular form of the bottleneck effect is called the founder effect. The founder effect occurs when a few individuals leave the population and colonize a new environment or become isolated in some way. The gene variations of the new population are not the same as those found in the population from which they separated. There is likely to be less genetic variety than there was in the original population, and this can lead to a high frequency of inherited disorders.

Approximately 30,000 people in South Africa carry the gene for the inherited blood disease porphyria. Each one is descended from the Dutch couple Ariaantje and Gerrit Jansz.

In the 1680s, Ariaantje and Gerrit Jansz emigrated from Holland to South Africa. Either Ariaantje or Gerrit suffered from a mild disease called porphyria. Porphyria is an inherited blood disease, and the gene for the disease was passed on to one or more of the couple's children. Today, more than 30,000 South Africans carry the porphyria gene. In every case that has been examined, it can be traced back to the Jansz couple. This is a remarkable example of the founder effect.

New Species

Natural selection, **mutations,** and **genetic drift** can all change the genetic make-up of a **population.** At what point do the changes become so great that the population becomes a separate **species?**

What is a species?

Individual members of a species can be strikingly different. A person might be short and fat with dark, curly hair, or tall and thin with straight, blond hair, yet both are obviously human. Members of a species can also look different at different stages in their lives. Think of the tadpole that becomes a frog or the maggot that becomes a fly. Differences in body form can be so great that we cannot use them as a means of defining a species.

Earlier, we defined a species as a group of organisms that can interbreed to produce fertile offspring. Dogs have been selectively bred by humans over many centuries so that now there are many different breeds. Yet all dogs are still members of the same species, because one breed can in theory mate with another, and the puppies they produce are capable of reproducing.

This is an eastern lowland gorilla (*Gorilla gorilla*). The eastern lowland and the mountain gorilla live in different habitats and eat different foods. With time, they will probably diverge to become separate species.

Isolation

A new species can arise if two populations of the same species living in different areas become isolated from each other. Two populations could become separated by a geographical obstacle, such as a mountain range. The isolated populations would begin to look and behave differently because random genetic changes and natural selection would shape the populations differently in different **habitats.** Such isolated populations of a species are called subspecies, and they can still interbreed. Eventually, however, they become so different that they are no longer the same species. Even if the geographical barriers between them were removed, they would no longer be able to interbreed. They would have diverged and changed to such an extent that they would become new species in their own right.

How many species?

No one has any idea how many species are living on the earth. Scientists have named roughly 1.8 million species. Guesses as to how many there really are range from 5 to 15 million. Insects are the most diverse species. They outnumber other species by more than 20 to 1. In 2000, a group of 40 scientists began the All Species Project. Their intention is to catalog every single species, from microbes to mammals, within 25 years.

Hybrids

It is sometimes possible for two species that are closely related to interbreed. The offspring that result are called hybrids. Hybrids are usually sterile, or unable to reproduce. A mule, which is a cross between a male donkey and a female horse, is an example of a hybrid.

Orchids form hybrids naturally. Gardeners have also created many beautiful artificial hybrids, such as this pansy orchid.

Barriers to breeding

Differences that evolve which prevent organisms from interbreeding with one another are called reproductive isolating mechanisms. Physical or behavioral differences may make mating impossible. For example, if one population does not recognize another's mating ritual, the two cannot mate. In some cases, the populations may be able to mate, but the sex cells are not compatible and fertilization does not occur.

4 A Tour of the Kingdoms

We have looked at some of the ways in which organisms can change and diversify. Over millions of years, these processes have resulted in the millions of different **species** that exist today. Now we can look more closely at the characteristics that distinguish each of the five **kingdoms** and the variety within each of these kingdoms.

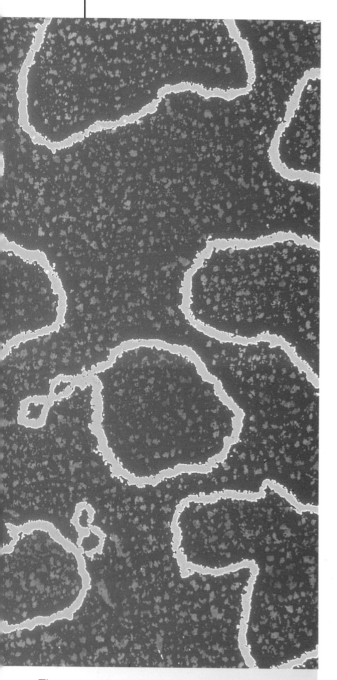

These are plasmids in the cytoplasm of *Escherichia coli*. Magnification approx. x 80,000.

Bacteria

Bacteria are microscopic single-celled organisms that are among the smallest living things. They are found almost everywhere. They are present in soil, air, and water under a wide range of conditions. Some bacteria are free living, while others are **parasites,** living on or in other living things. Many bacteria are **heterotrophs** and they need a food source. But there are also **autotrophic** bacteria. Some parasitic bacteria cause disease by producing toxins, or poisonous substances. Others are harmless, and still others even benefit their hosts. There are ten times more bacterial cells than human cells in the human body.

Bacteria are the oldest organisms. The oldest **fossils** known, nearly 3.5 billion years old, are fossils of bacteria-like organisms.

Bacterial structure

Each bacterium has an outer membrane, surrounded by a protective cell wall. The cell wall is made up of a complex mixture of **proteins, lipids,** and sugars. Some bacteria have the additional protection of a slime capsule that surrounds the cell wall.

Inside, the bacterial cell lacks structure. Bacteria have a large loop of **DNA,** sometimes called a bacterial chromosome, that is coiled up in one part of the **cytoplasm.** The DNA is attached to the cell membrane, but it is not separated from the rest of the cell inside a **nucleus.** In addition, bacteria often contain small, circular pieces of DNA known as **plasmids.** These plasmids can readily move from one bacterium to another, even though the bacteria may be different species. Some plasmids give the bacteria resistance to **antibiotics** that normally kill bacteria. The rapid spread of antibiotic resistance, which is of great concern to doctors, is passed from bacterium to bacterium by plasmid transfer. The cytoplasm may also contain granules of glycogen (a type of **carbohydrate**), lipids, or other food stores.

Bacteria usually reproduce by binary fission, dividing into two equal parts. Under ideal conditions, some bacteria can divide every twenty minutes. In most situations, limitations of food supply or space mean that growth is much slower.

Classifying bacteria

No one has any real idea how many species of bacteria there might be. About 4,000 species have been described and identified, but bacteriologists believe that the total number probably runs into the millions. Using a technique that involves the analysis of DNA, scientists recently estimated that there were 4,000 to 5,000 species of bacteria in a single gram of soil from a Norwegian beech forest.

The various shapes of bacteria are used as a method of classification. For example, cocci are round or oval bacteria, bacilli are rodlike, spirilla are spiral-shaped, and vibrios are shaped like commas.

An estimated 99 percent of bacteria lives in complex colonies called biofilms. These are made up of a number of different species of bacteria living together on a protective layer of slime.

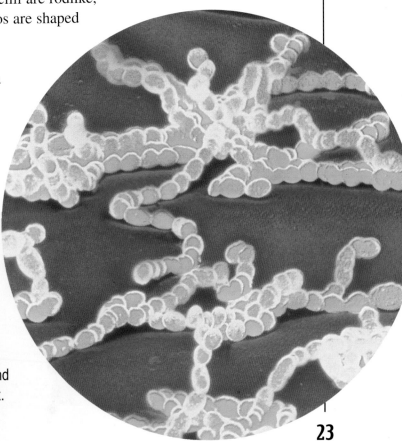

The oval shape of these bacteria identifies them as cocci. In this case, they are streptococci, bacteria that live in the mouths and noses of humans, horses, pigs, cows, and many other animals. Some species can cause serious sore throats, scarlet fever, and other diseases. Magnification approx. x 5,000.

Protistans

Protistans are difficult to classify. There are approximately 90,000 known living **species** of these organisms. Most of them are microscopic and single celled. They can be roughly divided into three main groups:

- plantlike protistans, the **algae**
- animal-like protistans, or **protozoans**
- funguslike protistans, such as water molds and slime molds.

Protistan cells are more structured than those of bacteria. Their **DNA** is separated from the rest of the **cytoplasm** inside a membrane-enclosed **nucleus.** For this reason, protistans and all other cells besides bacteria are called **eukaryotes,** which means "true nucleus." They also possess other cell structures, such as the mitochondria, where **respiration** takes place. The cells of algae, similar to those of plants, contain **chloroplasts,** which is where **photosynthesis** takes place.

The protistans come in a wide variety of forms and shapes. Some form colonies made up of many identical cells, while others such as the seaweeds are multicellular. Giant kelp, the largest kind of seaweed, may be 330 feet (100 meters) long. At the other end of the scale, some protozoan **parasites** are small enough to invade the cells of other organisms.

Plantlike protistans

Most algae live in water, although a few live in damp places on land, such as the surface of moist soil, on damp rocks, and on tree trunks. Seaweeds are the most obvious algae in the oceans. In some areas, giant kelp form underwater forests. However tiny, single-celled algae are a much more important part of life in the ocean. These tiny plantlike organisms are collectively known as phytoplankton.

Giant kelp is found off the west coast. Dense forests of kelp grow every spring then die back to nothing in the winter.

Almost all living creatures in the ocean depend either directly or indirectly on phytoplankton for their food. Many marine animals graze on these tiny algae, and they are in turn eaten by other animals. Phytoplankton are the first link in the ocean **food chain.**

Animal-like protistans

The animal-like protistans are sometimes called protozoans, which means "first animals." Protozoans are found everywhere there is moisture, including in the ocean and fresh water, in damp soil, and inside the moist interior of other organisms.

This is the single-celled, animal-like protistan *Amoeba proteus*. The fingerlike projections of the cytoplasm are called pseudopodia (false feet). Two can be seen on the left of this amoeba. Magnification approx. x 260.

Like animals, protozoans are **heterotrophs.** They must eat food in order to live. They move actively through their environment in search of nutrition. Some are grazers, some are predators, and some are parasites. **Amoebas** are protozoans that are very common in soil and water. They move around by forming projections called pseudopods (false feet). Most amoebas feed by completely surrounding their prey—usually smaller protozoans or algae—with pseudopodia and engulfing them. The digested prey is absorbed into the cell, and any indigestible material is expelled.

The Ciliophora, or ciliated protozoans, have numerous tiny hairlike structures called cilia on their surfaces. The cilia can beat back and forth like thousands of tiny oars, pushing the protozoans through their watery environment. The cilia also move food particles into the cell. Ciliophora prey on bacteria, algae, and each other.

The sporozoans are parasitic protozoans that complete part of their life cycle inside other cells. The most well-known example is *Plasmodium,* the organism that causes malaria. *Plasmodium* spends part of its life cycle in the *Anopheles* mosquito and part in the human liver and blood cells.

Funguslike protistans

Plasmodial slime molds are huge single cells fused together. Each cell has thousands of nuclei. Cellular slime molds usually exist as amoeba-like individuals. They join together in a swarm in response to a chemical signal.

Fungi

The fungi include familiar organisms such as mushrooms, puffballs, and toadstools, as well as the single-celled yeasts and the true molds. Unlike plants, fungi do not have chlorophyll in their cells or any other means of making their own food. Many fungi feed on dead and decaying animals or plants. Others are **parasites** that feed on living plants or animals. Some fungi live in or on plants in a **symbiotic** relationship, in which both organisms benefit from the association.

We know from **fossil** evidence that the first fungi evolved more than 900 million years ago. They made their first appearance on land along with plants, about 430 million years ago. About 100 million years after this, the three great groups of fungi were established: the zygomycetes (molds), sac fungi (such as truffles), and the club fungi (mushrooms and toadstools).

Alongside the bacteria, fungi are key members of the living world's clean-up squad. They are responsible for the decomposition, or rotting, of matter that was once alive. This decomposition releases valuable nutrients for recycling that would otherwise remain locked away in the bodies of dead organisms.

Fungal cells

Fungi are **eukaryotes,** and like plants, they have cell walls. The wall of a fungal cell may contain cellulose, similar to that of a plant cell. It may also contain another **carbohydrate** called chitin, which is similar to cellulose but not found in plant cells. Chitin is the main material in the hard outer skeletons of insects and spiders. Most fungi are composed of thin, microscopic filaments,

Yeast cells reproduce by budding. Budding is occurring in the two yeast cells in the center of this picture. Magnification approx. x 6,000.

called **hyphae,** that can grow rapidly. A network of hyphae, spreading through a food source, forms a **mycelium,** which is the body of a fungus. The hyphae form a complex system of microscopic tubes lined with **cytoplasm.** Although some **species** of fungus have incomplete cross walls that divide the hyphae into cell-like compartments, the hyphae are not clearly divided into individual cells. Each compartment may contain more than one **nucleus,** and cytoplasm is free to move from one compartment to another. This means that nutrients can flow freely through the mycelium.

Growing fungal hyphae produce **enzymes** that digest their food outside the body of the fungus. The fungus then absorbs the digested material. Fungi such as rots, that live on dead wood, can produce enzymes that break down the cellulose walls of the plant cells but have no effect on the chitin walls of the fungus.

Fungal reproduction

The mushrooms and toadstools that we see above ground are actually the reproductive **organs** of fungi growing beneath the surface. The underside of a mushroom's cap is lined with gills, or fine sheets of **tissue**, and it is here that the fungus produces spores. These spores are the reproductive cells of the fungus. Fungi produce spores in vast numbers. A melon-sized giant puffball can produce 70 trillion spores, each of which can potentially give rise to a new mycelium. Spores are light enough to be carried away from the parent fungus by air currents. If a spore lands on a suitable food source, it will grow and form a new mycelium.

Mold fungi, such as those that grow on decaying food, do not form mushroom-like reproductive structures. Instead, they send hyphae straight up from the mycelium. These swell at the top to produce spores. In yeasts, a cell produces a small growth, or bud. The bud gets larger and larger and eventually breaks away from the parent cell to become a new cell in its own right.

Spore production and budding are both forms of **asexual reproduction.** However, most fungi also have a sexual means of reproduction at some point in their lives. If the hyphae of two fungi of the same species meet, they may fuse together. This can result in a new mycelium that has **genetic material** from each of the fungi.

Bracket fungi grow on dead tree trunks, but they can also be found on live trees whose bark has been damaged in some way. The hyphae are hidden from view in the tree's bark, and the brackets are only produced when the fungi is about to reproduce.

Plants

Plants are a large and diverse group of organisms. They make their food through the process of **photosynthesis.** Photosynthesis involves capturing energy from sunlight and using it to build sugars from carbon dioxide and water. Because they can do this, plants have no need to move around in search of food and are adapted to a stationary lifestyle. This is reflected in the organization of a typical plant. Plants are usually made up of an above-ground shoot system for capturing light and making food, and a below-ground root system for absorbing water and **minerals** from the soil. Most plants are vascular, which means they have internal, tubelike **tissues** that carry nutrients, water, and minerals to all parts of the plant.

Plant groups

Plants can be divided into four main **phyla,** also known as divisions. The vast majority of plants are classified as **angiosperms,** the flowering, seed-bearing plants. Of the nearly 300,000 known **species** of plants, some 260,000 are angiosperms. The angiosperms are divided into two major **classes.** The dicotyledons produce seeds that contain an **embryo** plant with two seed leaves called cotyledons. They have broad leaves with branched veins. Most herbaceous plants, such as lettuce, daisies, and flowering shrubs, trees, and cacti, are dicotyledons. The monocotyledons have seeds that contain a single seed leaf. The mature plants have narrow leaves with straight, parallel veins. Orchids, lilies, palms, and grasses such as rice, wheat, and corn are all monocotyledons.

The **gymnosperms** are shrubs or trees that form so-called naked seeds. The most abundant of these plants are conifer trees, such as firs, spruces, redwoods, and pine trees. There are about 750 species of gymnosperms.

In this picture of a moss (*Polytrichum commune*), the yellow capsules and long stalks form the sporophytes. Mosses are members of the **bryophyte** division, one of the four main phyla in the plant **kingdom.**

28

Flowering plants evolved only about 135 million years ago, which is quite recent in the history of life. Today, they are the most widespread plant group on Earth. This is an oak tree.

Ferns, of which there are about 12,000 species, have roots and stems but do not flower. They produce spores on the undersides of their leaflike fronds.

The second largest plant division is the bryophytes. It includes mosses, **liverworts,** and **hornworts.** The bryophytes are nonvascular. They grow low to the ground and have leaflike, stemlike, and rootlike parts. They have none of the complex tissues found in flowering plants. There are about 19,000 bryophyte species.

Deep Green

At a science conference in 1999, a group of scientists reported the results of a six-year project called Deep Green. The aim of Deep Green was to sort and classify all the known species of green plants. They suggested that plants be divided into three kingdoms rather than one, discovered the most primitive living flowering plant species, and possibly identified the "mother" of all green plant species.

The scientists put together evolutionary histories of flowering plants based on their **DNA,** put them into a rough time order based on their **mutations,** and revealed that a rare tropical shrub called *Amborella*, found only in the South Pacific, is the closest living relative of the first flowering plant.

The Deep Green study also supported the idea that single-celled **algae** evolved into mosses at least 450 million years ago and became the first land plants. DNA data suggest that the green plants which first took root on land are most closely related to certain species of algae that are still abundant today.

Plant Evolution

The ancestors of plants probably evolved in Earth's oceans from simple **eukaryote** cells about 700 million years ago. Every plant in the world today is descended from green **algae** that lived along Earth's ancient shores.

From water to land

More than 250 million more years passed before the first simple plants began establishing themselves on land. As they did, they developed simple structures that gave them a firm attachment in their new environment. Eventually, these structures developed into root systems.

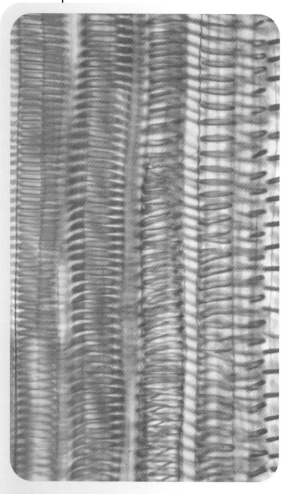

Xylem vessels are modified cells that carry water around plants. Their walls are thickened by spiral bands of lignin (stained blue) that support the plant. Magnification approx. x 5,500.

The aboveground shoot systems were at first only branched stems with spines. Later plants developed the primary **organs** for **photosynthesis,** the leaves. At some point plants evolved the ability to make lignin, a waterproofing, strengthening material that was deposited in their cell walls. The additional strength this gave allowed for the development of stems that could support leaves and position them in the best way to gather light.

Plants also began to develop efficient transport systems to carry water, dissolved **minerals,** and nutrients throughout the plant. There are two types of these pipelines. Phloem cells carry sugars from the leaves to the rest of the plant. Xylem cells bring water and minerals up from the roots. The phloem and xylem running through the leaves also act as a skeletal system, providing strength and allowing for the growth of leaves that are larger than would otherwise be possible.

Another necessity for life on land is the conservation of water. To meet this demand, plants evolved a waxy covering called the **cuticle.** The cuticle protects the plant's shoots and helps prevent them from drying out. However, tiny openings in the surface of a leaf, called stomata, allow carbon dioxide to be absorbed for the purposes of photosynthesis.

Reproduction

As plants moved out across the land, their life cycles began to change. Algae, the plantlike **protistans,** need liquid water in order to reproduce. On land there is no guarantee that water will be available at any given time, and a stationary plant cannot go off in search of it. In fact, the lack of water must have favored the development of plants with extensive root systems. These plants could take as much water as possible from the soil. At some point in their life cycle, plants form sex cells, but in flowering plants these cells do not need water to reproduce.

Flowering plants have developed two distinct forms of sex cells. They are the female egg cells, found inside the ovules, and the male sex cells, formed inside pollen. The **evolution** of lightweight pollen grains has allowed flowering plants to spread widely. Pollen grains allow the plant to get male sex cells to the eggs without water.

In some groups of flowering plants, the pollen is carried by the wind. Other plants have evolved partnerships with animals, usually insects. In these partnerships, the animal visits the plant for food and in return carries pollen to other plants. Flowering plants have evolved various large, colorful, scented flowers that contain sugary nectar to attract insects and other animals.

Seeds have also contributed to the plant **kingdom's** successful colonization of the land. Seeds are formed by the fertilized plant. They contain an **embryo** plant inside a tough, waterproof seed coat. This prevents it from drying out. The seed contains nutrients to give the new plant a good start in life.

The seeds of dandelions (*Taraxacum* species) are attached to tiny parachutes which help carry them away from the parent plant in a gust of wind.

31

The most familiar animals, such as fish, amphibians, reptiles, birds, and mammals, are all vertebrates, or animals with backbones. However, they form only a tiny part of the animal **kingdom.** More than two million **species** of animal have been identified, most of which are invertebrates, or animals without backbones. Fewer than 50,000 species are classed as vertebrates.

Animal characteristics

All animals are multicellular. In most cases, the cells that comprise an animal's body are divided into **tissues,** groups of similar cells that work together to perform a particular job. Examples are muscle tissue or nervous tissue. Groups of tissues are arranged together to form the **organs** of the animal, such as the heart and liver. All animals consume and digest food in order to obtain their nutrition. Because they need to find food, most animals can move around for at least part of their life cycle.

Invertebrates

Sponges (Porifera) are among the earliest and simplest of the animal groups. They live in the ocean or in fresh water. Unlike other animals, sponges do not have mouths. Small holes or pores on the sponge draw water into a central cavity. The water then escapes through larger openings. Sponge **fossils** have been found from the **Precambrian era,** more than 550 million years ago.

Jellyfish and corals (Cnidaria) are a varied group of mostly marine animals that are armed with stinging cells. They probably evolved a few million years after the sponges.

Barnacles such as this acorn barnacle (*Balanus balanoides*) feed by catching food particles carried in the water, so they do not need to move about. However, young barnacles are different from adults. They must swim around for food.

Flatworms (Platyhelminthes) are simple animals whose bodies have just three layers of cells. This makes them generally long and flat. They include flatworms, tapeworms, and blood flukes.

Roundworms (Nematoda) are wormlike animals whose bodies are long and threadlike. There are more than 15,000 known species.

Starfish and sea urchins (Echinodermata) are all ocean-living animals that often have tough, spiny skin. They go back more than 500 million years ago.

Mollusks (Mollusca) include snails, clams, mussels, oysters, squid, and octopuses. They often have hard outer shells. There are more than 50,000 species.

Segmented worms (Annelida) include earthworms and their relatives, leeches, and a large number of marine worms known as polychaetes. Some live in the soil, some live in the ocean, and some are **parasites.** Their bodies are made up of separate segments.

Arthropods (Arthropoda) include insects, spiders, scorpions, and crustaceans such as crabs and shrimps. About 80 percent of animals are arthropods, and the majority of arthropods are insects. There are more insect species than all other animals put together. Arthropods have jointed limbs and a hard outer skeleton, called an exoskeleton, that they shed at intervals as they grow.

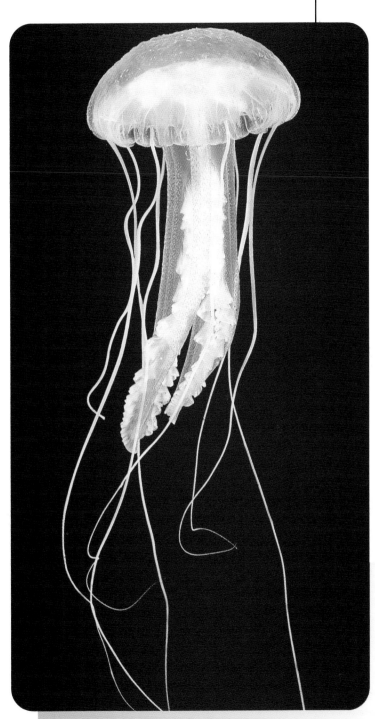

This jellyfish (*Pelaga noctiluca*) feeds by paralyzing its prey with tiny stinging cells on its eight tentacles.

Animals: Vertebrates

Vertebrates have a history on Earth of more than 500 million years. The first vertebrates were jawless fish, similar to today's hagfish and lampreys. **Fossils** of jawed vertebrates appeared about 100 million years later.

A vertebrate is distinguished from other animals by its backbone. This segmented column can be made of **cartilage** or bone and protects the spinal cord. The brain is protected inside a bony skull. Other features of vertebrates include a relatively well developed brain, paired complex eyes, a muscular mouth, and a well-developed circulatory system with a heart.

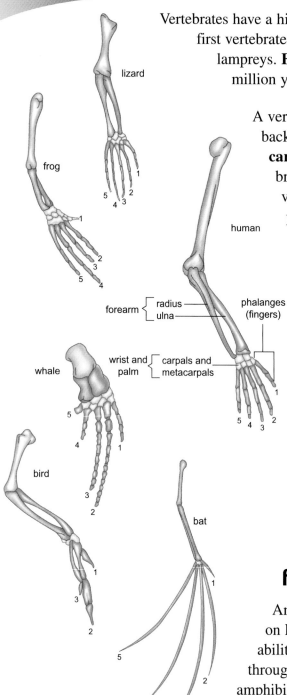

Fish

There are three main fish **classes:** the jawless fish; the cartilaginous fish, whose skeleton is made of cartilage; and the bony fish. The jawless fish are the oldest vertebrates. The cartilaginous fish include the sharks, skates, and rays. Instead of scales, their skin is covered in tiny, toothlike structures called denticles.

Nearly all other fish—more than 20,000 known **species**—are bony fish. Bony fish first evolved about 130 million years ago. Today, they dominate the ocean. They come in a huge variety of forms and sizes and live in a wide range of **habitats.**

Amphibians

Amphibians spend part of their lives in water and part on land. They can do this because they have a unique ability to breathe in both places. In water, they breathe through their smooth, scaleless skin. On land, most amphibians breathe through lungs. Frogs, toads, and newts are the best-known amphibians.

Reptiles

Reptiles are cold-blooded animals. They were the first of the true land-living vertebrates. They did not return to water to breed. The earliest fossil reptile is a tiny, lizardlike creature from almost 350 million years ago called *Petrolacosaurus*. There are nearly 8,000 known modern reptiles, including crocodiles, lizards, snakes, and turtles. They have scaly skin and lay eggs that have leathery shells.

Land vertebrates have characteristic pentadactyl, or five-fingered, limbs. The limbs have evolved in different ways in different species.

Birds

Birds are land-living animals that breathe through lungs and maintain a constant body temperature. They all have wings and feathers, and most can fly. Birds have beaks for feeding and lay eggs encased in hard shells. There are about 9,000 species of birds. They probably evolved from small dinosaurs more than 200 million years ago.

Mammals

Mammals are more intelligent than other animals. Like birds, they maintain a constant body temperature despite changes in the temperature of their surroundings. Nearly all mammals have hair or fur, and the young feed on their mother's milk. There are approximately 4,500 mammal species, of which 4,000 are placental mammals. Placental mammals produce live young that are nourished in the mother's womb through a specialized **organ** called the placenta. Placental mammals range in size from shrews to whales and include dogs, cats, sheep, cattle, and humans.

Marsupials are the second largest mammal group. They include all of the pouched animals, such as opossums, kangaroos, and koala bears. Marsupial babies are born tiny and helpless, then grow and develop in their mother's pouch. The third group, the monotremes, are mammals that lay eggs rather than give birth to live young. The best-known monotreme is the duck-billed platypus. Another is the echinda.

A female red deer (*Cervus elaphus*) feeds her young. Mammals are the only animals that produce milk for their young.

5 A Brief History of Life

Scientists have learned a lot about the history of life by examining **fossil** records. However, there is still so much we do not know. We have no animal fossils from more than about 600 million years ago, yet it was a long time before this that something very important happened on this planet. Life appeared.

Most scientists believe that the first life-forms appeared on Earth as much as four billion years ago, just 500 million years after Earth itself was formed. It seems that life appeared on the scene just as soon as it could. The first recognizable fossils appear to be from around 3.5 billion years ago, and there are traces of life dating as far back as 3.7 to 3.8 billion years ago. In fact, there is no evidence that life didn't appear more than once, only to be wiped out by an **asteroid** impact and reappear later. Every organism on Earth today can trace its ancestry back to a survivor of those early days.

Earliest life

Evolution can't tell us how life first appeared. Evolution is only concerned with what happened to life afterward—how it changed and evolved. The first cells were relatively simple, perhaps similar to today's bacteria. The environment they found themselves in was harsh. For one thing, there was no ozone layer to block the sun's ultraviolet (UV) radiation, and this would have resulted in many **mutations** in the bacterial **DNA.** These mutations would have been a factor in driving the evolution of the first cells.

Not long after life began, the bacteria diverged into two great groups: the eubacteria and the **archaebacteria.** Not long after this, the **eukaryotes** evolved from the archaebacteria. The ancestors of today's multicelled life may have been very similar to the extremophiles, bacteria that thrive in hot springs at temperatures of 235°F (113°C) or more and around ocean-floor volcanic vents.

Changes in Earth's atmosphere were important in establishing life on our planet.

A change in the atmosphere

Eventually, bacteria emerged that could use the energy of the sun to make food through the process of **photosynthesis.** This was a major leap forward in the history of life, and here's why. Oxygen is a byproduct of photosynthesis. With bacteria now photosynthesizing, oxygen slowly accumulated in the atmosphere over hundreds of millions of years. And this had two effects. First, oxygen accumulated in the upper atmosphere as ozone and blocked harmful UV radiation. Second, organisms evolved a way to use oxygen to obtain energy from their food more efficiently than ever before.

It took a long time for single-celled life to evolve into more complex multicellular organisms. Today, our best guess is that multicelled life did not appear until about 1,500 million years ago, or about 2,500 million years after life first appeared. This suggests that it was a very difficult step for life to take. Perhaps it was necessary for photosynthesis and **respiration** to evolve first. Then life began to take off, spreading out and diversifying into all of the environments that young Earth had to offer.

Stromatolites are rocklike structures built from deposits trapped by photosynthetic bacteria. Stromatolite fossils have been found in rocks that are 3 billion years old.

An Explosion of Life

Our picture of the past is very incomplete. Only those organisms that had hard body parts, that happened to be buried in just the right circumstances for **fossil** formation, and that happened to have been dug up by fossil hunters play a part in this story. Scientists believe that fewer than four percent of the organisms that have lived have left a fossil record.

By the end of the **Precambrian era,** 570 million years ago, the world was rich in life, but we have no record of what that life was like. The fossil record for this period is extremely poor. We know that there were **protistans,** fungi, and animals, although there were not any plants. Most of the major animal forms evolved for the first time in the seas of the **Cambrian** era that followed. Many of these early **species** probably lived in sediments rich in **organic** remains that drifted down to the seafloors. These primitive animals were extremely diverse.

The great diversification that took place roughly 530 million years ago is sometimes called the big bang of animal **evolution,** or the Cambrian explosion. The reasons for this outpouring of life-forms are not entirely clear. Some scientists would dispute that there was an explosion at all. Remember, we know very little of what was going on before this period.

One reason for the sudden diversity was probably competition. Animals were competing with each other as predators and prey, and they evolved new ways of attack and defense. Then, as now, the race between predator and prey was one of the greatest spurs to evolution.

Colonizing the land

The Cambrian explosion took place entirely in the water. During this period, the land was lifeless and empty. By about 450 million years ago, some areas may have supported a few **lichens.** On the margins of rivers, there were probably some green **algae.** It is from these freshwater algae that land plants are thought to have developed.

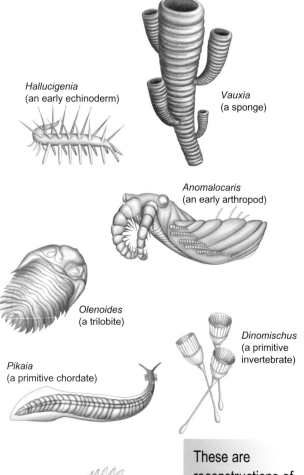

Hallucigenia
(an early echinoderm)

Vauxia
(a sponge)

Anomalocaris
(an early arthropod)

Olenoides
(a trilobite)

Dinomischus
(a primitive invertebrate)

Pikaia
(a primitive chordate)

Canadia
(a polychaete worm)

These are reconstructions of some of the life-forms that appeared during the Cambrian explosion.

Land animals

As plants began to colonize the land, animals followed. The earliest animal colonizers were **arthropods** such as spiders and millipedes. Then about 360 million years ago, new animals, the **tetrapods,** began to colonize the land. These animals evolved from fish and diversified into the amphibians, reptiles, birds, and mammals we see today. However, just like modern amphibians, the early tetrapods needed to return to the water to breed. To be true land animals, they had to develop a way to reproduce without water.

This step came with the evolution of the reptiles. They laid eggs that were protected from drying out by a leathery shell. Inside the egg, the developing **embryo** grows in its own pool, protected by a membrane called the amnion. Because of this feature, reptiles and the other land-living animals that descended from them, the birds and mammals, are called **amniotes.** No longer dependent on staying near a water supply, the amniotes could spread out across the earth.

This fossil of the plant *Archaefructus liaoningensis* is currently the oldest flowering plant fossil known. It was found in China in rocks about 140 million years old. The plant does not have obvious flowers or fruits. The plant's seeds are contained in folded leaves.

6 The End of the Line

The history of life has not been a smooth progression from simple life-forms to more complex ones. No **species** lasts forever. **Evolution** is about change, and one species gives way to another that is better adapted to the surroundings. Some groups of living things, such as the dinosaurs, were very successful. Yet individual dinosaur species still came and then vanished again. On average, a species lasts between two and ten million years, and the vast majority of species that have ever lived are now extinct. When a species becomes extinct, its particular combination of **genes** are removed forever from life's pool of diversity.

Trilobites were a hugely successful group of **arthropods.** For 300 million years from the **Cambrian** era onward, they lived in the ancient ocean. Then 250 million years ago, at the end of the Permian period, all trilobites became extinct.

Many things can cause a species to become extinct. A species may die out because another species outcompetes it, for example. Survival of the fittest doesn't just apply to individual members within a species, but also to species themselves. Perhaps as a result of inbreeding, a species might lack the genetic diversity to adapt to changing circumstances, such as a cooling climate or the arrival of a new predator. Many extinctions are the result of a newly evolved species replacing its ancestors because the new species is better adapted to the environment.

Individual extinctions have occurred throughout the history of life. There is an estimated rate of extinction of roughly one to two species per year. However, at certain points in the past there have been mass extinctions, when many species were wiped out all at once as the result of a natural catastrophe such as an **asteroid** strike or a major shift in the climate.

Extinction and evolution

Extinction has played a major role in the evolution of life on Earth. The **fossil** record that stretches back more than 600 million years shows that there have been four or five mass extinctions. The greatest known extinction episode took place some 250 million years ago at the end of the **Permian period,** when 95 percent of all marine species and 50 percent of land species were wiped out. At this time, Earth was going through a period of major geological and climate changes which were probably the main cause of the extinctions.

The extinction of one species may represent an opportunity for a new species to come along and occupy the **habitat** left empty by the vanished species. A mass extinction is an opportunity for **adaptive radiation** and the appearance of many new species. The dinosaurs, one of the most successful of all animal groups, began to rise to dominance after a mass extinction and the breakup of the supercontinent of **Pangaea** opened new habitats.

Another example of a mass extinction opening new habitats for the survivors has already been discussed. The ancestors of today's mammals lived alongside the dinosaurs for tens of millions of years. All of the major habitats were filled by the dinosaurs, and the mammals could not compete with them. The first mammals were small animals that made their living as scavengers. Within about ten million years of the dinosaurs' extinction, all of the major **orders** of mammals and birds had emerged. Both groups had evolved and adapted to occupy the roles that the dinosaurs had left empty.

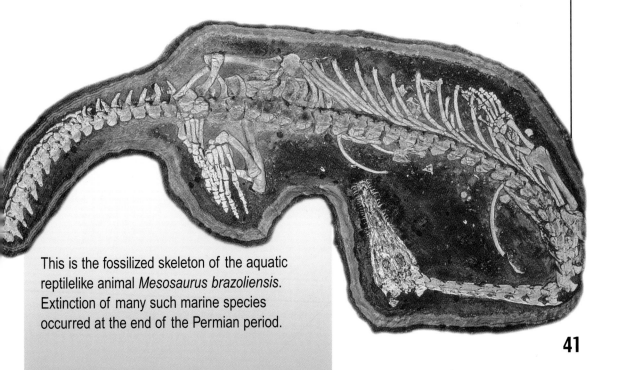

This is the fossilized skeleton of the aquatic reptilelike animal *Mesosaurus brazoliensis*. Extinction of many such marine species occurred at the end of the Permian period.

The Threat to Diversity

Twelve thousand years ago, North America had a spectacular range of large animals. They included condors with a wingspan of almost sixteen feet (five meters), three kinds of elephants, eight kinds of big cats, long-legged pigs, giant wolves, and giant armadillos. There were more big animal **species** than you can find today in Africa.

Then, 11,000 years ago, 95 percent of these big animals disappeared completely. This event coincided with another major change in the area—the arrival of human beings. It may not have been entirely human hunters who caused these extinctions. Climate change may have played a part as well. However, the speed of the extinctions and the fact that many of the species had previously survived ice ages, suggest that it was humans who tipped the balance.

A mass extinction of Earth's organisms is now under way, and the cause of it is the human race. Since the invention of agriculture about 10,000 years ago and with increasing speed over the last 200 years, we have been changing the face of the Earth. The land and ocean, the atmosphere, and probably the climate have all been affected. Human activities are changing the environment and in turn changing the conditions in which other organisms have to live. Mammals survived the catastrophe that wiped out the dinosaurs, but today more than 300 of the 4,500 or so mammal species are threatened by extinction as a result of human activity. More than two-thirds of the known bird species are threatened by the loss of **habitat.** Rates of extinction are likely to continue increasing as the human **population** increases, putting greater and greater pressure on natural resources.

The Tasmanian Wolf, or thylacine (*Thylacinus cynocephalus*) is a dog-like marsupial thought to be extinct. Its numbers decreased following the introduction of dogs to Tasmania.

A modern catastrophe

Extinctions that result from human activity have several different causes and some are more obvious than others. Some species have been hunted to extinction. The passenger pigeon existed in huge numbers in eastern North America. However, early settlers killed so many of these birds that by the end of the nineteenth century the population had declined from billions of birds to zero. Less well known is the fact that two species of lice that were dependent on the bird became extinct, too.

A more important cause of extinctions today is the loss of habitat. Habitat destruction worldwide is taking place at a tremendous rate. The losses are greatest in tropical rain forests, where the diversity of species is also highest. More than half of these rain forests have already been cut down for timber and farming.

Another human cause of extinctions has been the introduction of non-native species into habitats. Many extinctions have taken place on islands, where species with no natural enemies are particularly at risk from the introduction of predators such as cats and rats that are brought in either accidentally or deliberately.

The next wave

After every mass extinction that has taken place over the long history of life on Earth, diversity has increased to a greater level than it was at previously. It is sobering to think that no matter what we do, we will not be able to stop life in its tracks. Not even the **asteroid** that shattered the dinosaurs' world could do that. There is greater diversity now than ever before, but it has taken a very long recovery time— 65 million years—for this diversity to evolve.

This region of Costa Rica was once rain forest, but the trees have been clear-cut and now cattle graze here. Clear-cutting of rain forests could cause a mass extinction.

The Kingdoms of Life

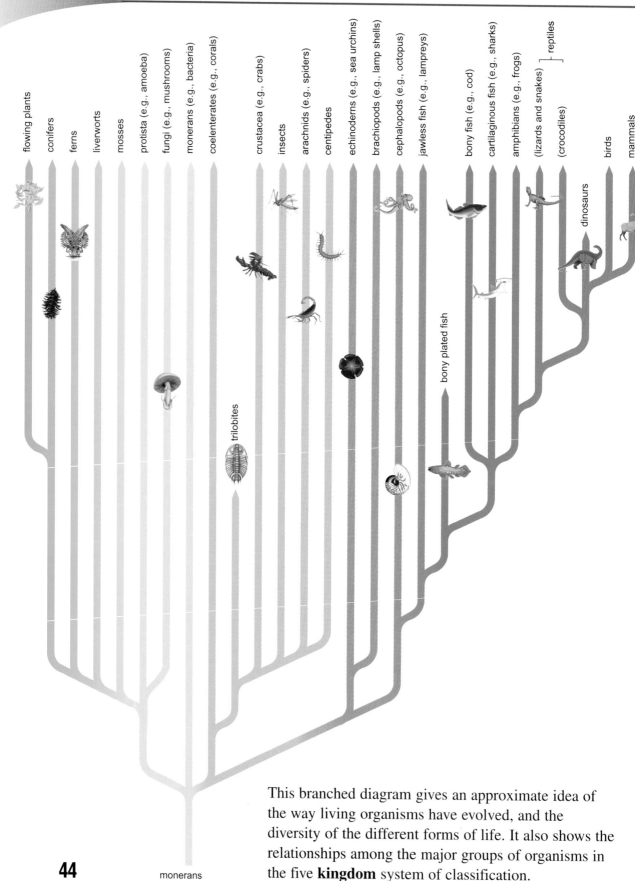

This branched diagram gives an approximate idea of the way living organisms have evolved, and the diversity of the different forms of life. It also shows the relationships among the major groups of organisms in the five **kingdom** system of classification.

Glossary

adaptive radiation development of many different species from a single ancestral group as organisms get used to different habitats or ways of life

alga (plural **algae**) see **Protista**.

amniote animal, such as a reptile, bird, or mammal that produces shelled eggs. Mammals are amniotes because the placenta is a structure evolved from the amniote egg.

amoeba (plural amoebae) single-celled, animal-like organism

angiosperm flowering plant

antibiotic synthetic drug or a chemical produced by a microorganism that kills bacteria

archaebacterium (plural archaebacteria) bacterial species considered by many scientists to be a separate kingdom, that are characteristically found in extreme environments, for example around volcanic springs and in salt lakes

arthropod invertebrate with jointed legs and a segmented body. Crustaceans, spiders, and insects are arthropods.

asexual reproduction single organism produces genetically identical copies, or clones, of itself

asteroid lump of rock that travels through space. It ranges from 0.6 to 621 miles (1 to 1,000 kilometers) in diameter.

autotroph organism that can make its own food

bryophyte small, simple, rootless plants

Cambrian geological period of time, 545 to 505 million years ago

carbohydrate chemical compound composed of carbon, hydrogen, and oxygen

Carnivora (carnivores) meat-eating mammals

cartilage stiff material, more flexible than bone, that is used as a supporting **tissue** in vertebrates

chloroplast structure found within plant cells where photosynthesis takes place

class grouping of organisms. A class is larger than an **order** but smaller than a phylum.

cuticle waxy layer on the surface of leaves that reduces water loss

cytoplasm all of the contents of a cell between the **nucleus** and the outer membrane

DNA (deoxyribonucleic acid) genetic material of living things. DNA carries instructions for constructing, maintaining, and reproducing living cells

embryo very young organism in the early stages of development, before it emerges from the egg or seed or is born from its mother

enzyme special protein that controls the speed of chemical reactions within the cell

eukaryote cell that contains a membrane-enclosed nucleus. All living things except bacteria are eukaryotes.

evolution changes in characteristics of groups of organisms over many generations

family grouping of organisms. A family is bigger than a **genus** but smaller than an order.

food chain relationships of organisms linked by the foods they eat

fossil organism, part of an organism, or traces of an organism preserved in rock

gene section of DNA that codes for a single protein or part of a protein. Genes are the basic units of heredity.

genetic drift change in the frequency of genes in populations by chance rather than by natural selection

genetic material the DNA found within each living cell that carries the instructions for creating a new organism

genus (plural genera) grouping of organisms. A genus is larger than a species but smaller than a family.

gymnosperma (gymnosperms) group of plants that includes conifer trees such as pines, spruces, and firs

herbivore animal that feeds only on plants

habitat place where an animal lives

heterotroph organism that needs an external source of food to survive. All animals are heterotrophs.

hornwort simple, green, leaflike plant similar to the liverwort

hypha (plural **hyphae**) thin, threadlike structure that forms the body of a fungus

kingdom largest grouping of organisms

lichen plantlike growth covering other plants or rocks

lipid oil, fat, wax, and other fatty substances

liverwort small, simple, leaflike plant found in wet places such as river banks and damp woods

mineral simple chemical substance required by living organisms

Monera kingdom that includes the most ancient organisms, including bacteria, blue-green algae, and viruses

mutation random change in an organism's genetic material

mycelium body of a fungus

nucleus large structure found in eukaryote cells that contains the cell's genetic material

order grouping of organisms. An order is larger than a family but smaller than a class.

organ collection of different tissues in an animal's body that work together to perform a function

organelle one of several different structures surrounded by a membrane found in eukaryote cells

organic anything related to or derived from living things

Pangaea supercontinent formed from all the present continents before they broke apart

parasite organism that lives in or on another organism, obtaining food from it without giving anything in return

Permian period geological period of time between 290 and 250 million years ago. The end of this period is marked by the Permian extinction, in which 95 percent of all marine animals died out.

photosynthesis process by which plants and algae make sugary food using energy from sunlight, carbon dioxide from the air, and water

phylum (plural **phyla**) largest grouping of organisms within a kingdom

plasmid small, circular piece of DNA found in bacterial cells

population group of organisms within a species that live together in a particular area

Precambrian era geological period before the Cambrian from about 4,000 million years ago to 545 million years ago

prokaryote cell that does not contain a nucleus. Bacteria are prokaryote cells.

protein substance that makes up many cell structures and controls a cell's reactions

Protista kingdom of eukaryote organisms, mostly single-celled. Some protistans, such as **protozoans,** have animal-like qualities, while others, such as algae, are more like plants.

protozoan see **Protista**

respiration process by which all organisms obtain energy from food by breaking down sugars into simpler substances

sexual reproduction sex cells from the father and the mother combine to form a cell that will grow into a new individual

species group of closely related living things that can breed together and produce fertile offspring

symbiotic any close relationship between two or more different species

taxonomy study of the classification of organisms

tetrapod any four-limbed vertebrate

tissue group of similar cells, all of which have a particular function in an organism

Further Reading

Burnie, David. *Eyewitness Guide: Life.* New York: Dorling Kindersley, 1998.

Parker, Steve. *Life Processes: Adaptations.* Chicago: Heinemann Library, 2001.

Parker, Steve. *Life Processes: Survival and Change.* Chicago: Heinemann Library, 2001.

Wallace, Holly. *Life Processes: Cells and Systems.* Chicago: Heinemann Library, 2001.

Wallace, Holly. *Life Processes: Classification.* Chicago: Heinemann Library, 2001.

Index